Nappy Nicky

Written by
Sunita Miya Muganza

Illustrated by
Emmanuel Gyamfi Boateng

Muganza, Sunita Miya

Illustrated by Emmanuel Gyamfi Boateng

ISBN: 978-1777823306 (Paperback)

ISBN: 978-1777823313 (eBook)

Printed in Canada

*I want to dedicate this book to the two
most important women I have ever known.
My Bibi and my mother Aziza Juma.
I am who I am because of you.*

Love Sunita,

Hi! My name is Wema Ninoshka Komba but you can call me Ninoshka. I'm excited to share my story with you as each word leads you from page to page.

My family and I are from *Uganda*. Uganda is pronounced "ooo-gan-dah", not "YOU-gan-dah". But Canada is now my second home. I speak two languages, *English and Swahili*, and I'm thrilled to teach you how to use a few fun Swahili words!

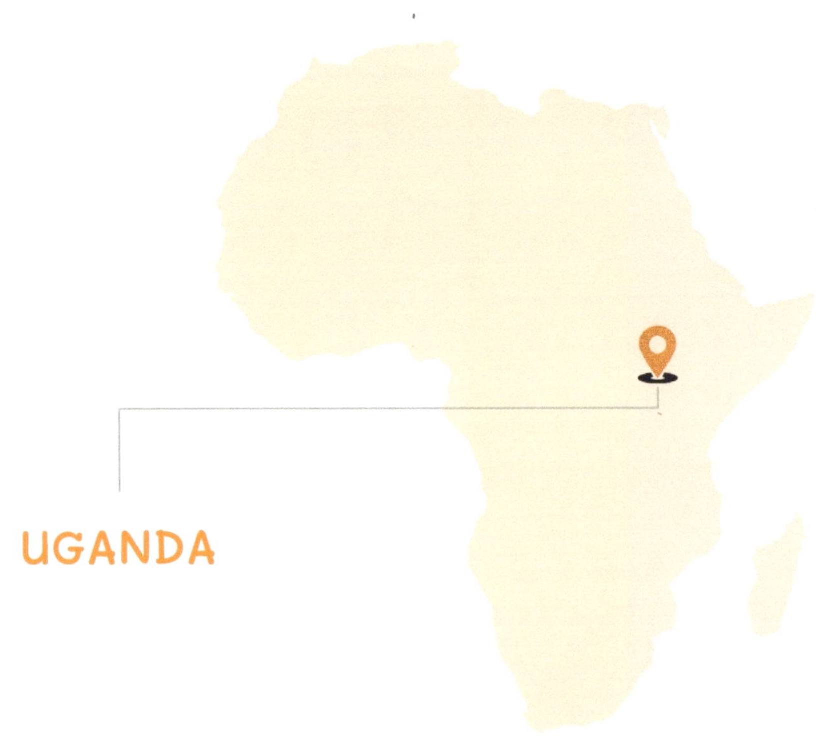

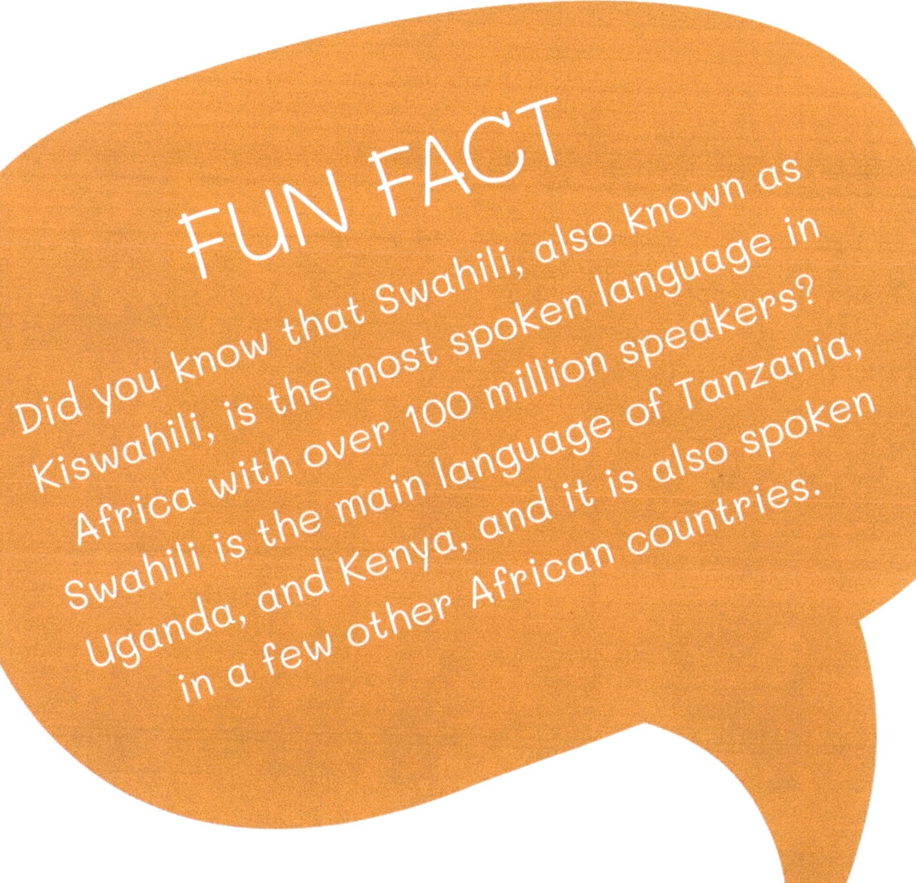

Here's a short list of some cool, new words you'll learn throughout the story!

	Meaning	Sounds like
Bibi	("Grandmother")	"Bee-bee"
Kaa	("Sit down")	"Kaah"
Apana	("No")	"Ah-paa-na"
Niambe	("Tell me")	"Nee-ah-mbee-yeh"
Pole	("Sorry")	"Po-leh"
Angalia Tena	("Look again")	"Ah-ga-lee-ah Teh-na"

BIG
BEAR

Ninoshka stood in front of
her tall, white oak mirror playing
with her bouncy coils. She grabbed
a spirally strand, stretched it down
her face, and watched the coil as it
straightened.

She smiled.

When she gently let go of the strand, her hair snapped back into a *kinky curl*.

She frowned.

"Ninoshka, Ninoshka!"
Bibi shouted warmly.

"Njoo hapa ('come here')!
It is time to do your hair."

"Is all of this for my hair?" she asked as her eyes wandered across the bathroom counter.

"Yes, kaa ('sit')," Bibi said softly.

Ninoshka sunk down onto the petite sitting stool and asked, "What are we doing to my hair?"

"I am going to deep condition and shampoo your hair, Ninoshka," Bibi answered.

Using a *wide-toothed comb*, Bibi parted Ninoshka's hair into large sections and braided each section neatly. Then Bibi began to apply a bottle of hot *Morrocan oil* to Ninoshka's scalp.

After Bibi was finished, she rested the warm oil bottle back on the counter.

As she waited, Ninoshka noticed a familiar green plant laying next to the other hair products on the counter.

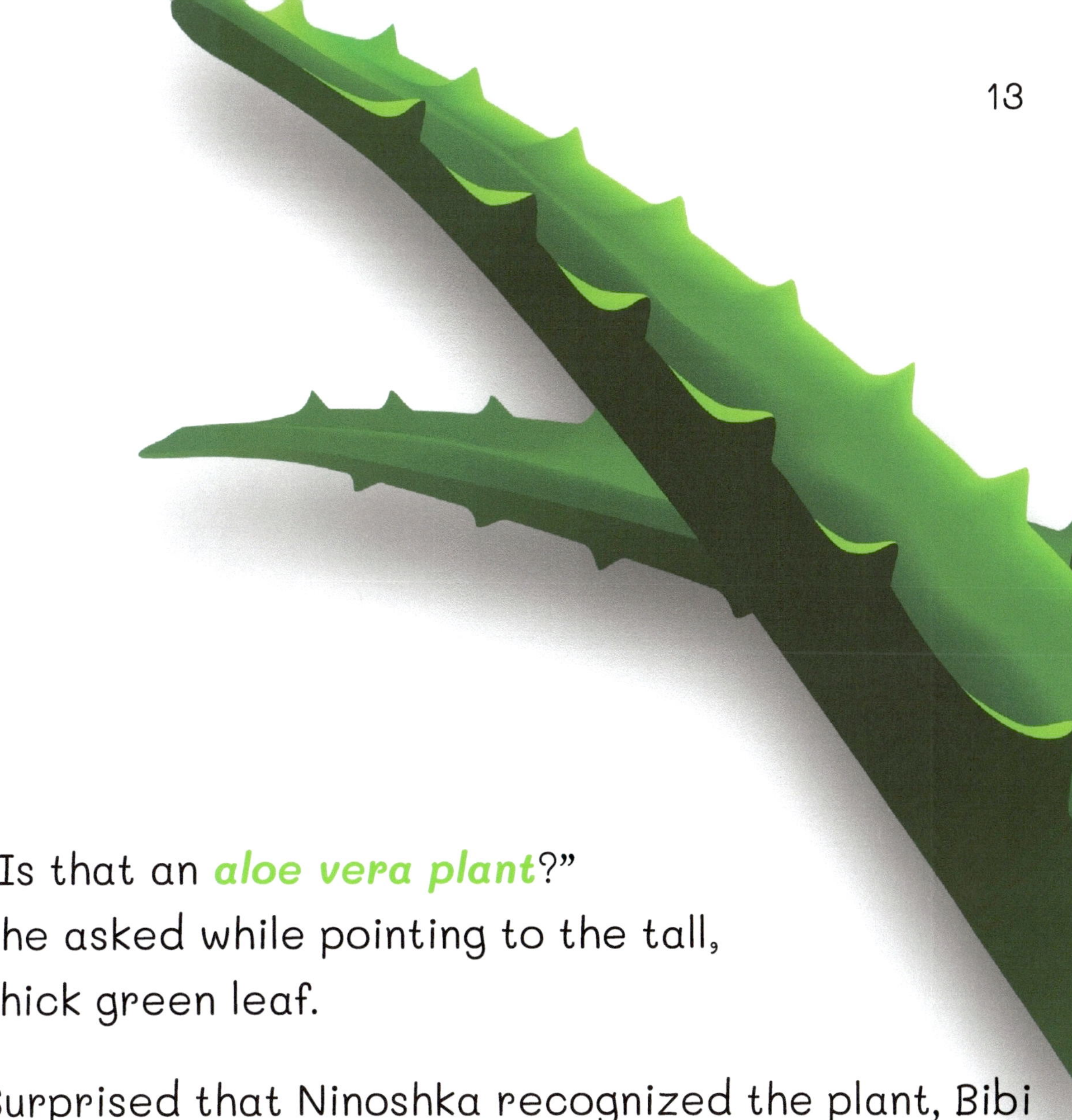

"Is that an *aloe vera plant*?"
he asked while pointing to the tall,
thick green leaf.

Surprised that Ninoshka recognized the plant, Bibi
exclaimed, "Yes, it is!"

Why are you using it in my hair?"
Ninoshka asked.

"The gel from the aloe vera plant can be used to condition and soften your hair. It also reduces dandruff and helps your hair grow. We have used the aloe plant in our family for years because it is an ancient beauty tradition!" Bibi explained.

Then Ninoshka asked, "Can it straighten my hair as well?"

"Apana ('no'), but I can use the aloe vera gel to soothe the bruises on your toes from ballet.

"Why do you ask?" Bibi questioned.

Ninoshka's face fell into a frown and she remained silent.

16

"Wema Ninoshka, niambe ('tell me').
Why do you want to straighten your
hair?"
Bibi asked again.

"They make fun of me," Ninoshka
whispered.

"Who makes fun of you?" asked Bibi.

"The other
ballerinas.
They call
me 'Nappy
Nicky',"
said
Ninoshka.

"Pole
('sorry'), my
love," Bibi said
softly.

17

"They say that my hair is **messy**, **wild**, and **unfit** for a ballerina. They make up silly songs about my hair and laugh at me after class," she whispered.

Last week, my hair was styled in an afro and one of the ballerinas grumbled to Ms. Taylor that my hair was blocking her view while we practiced our pliers.

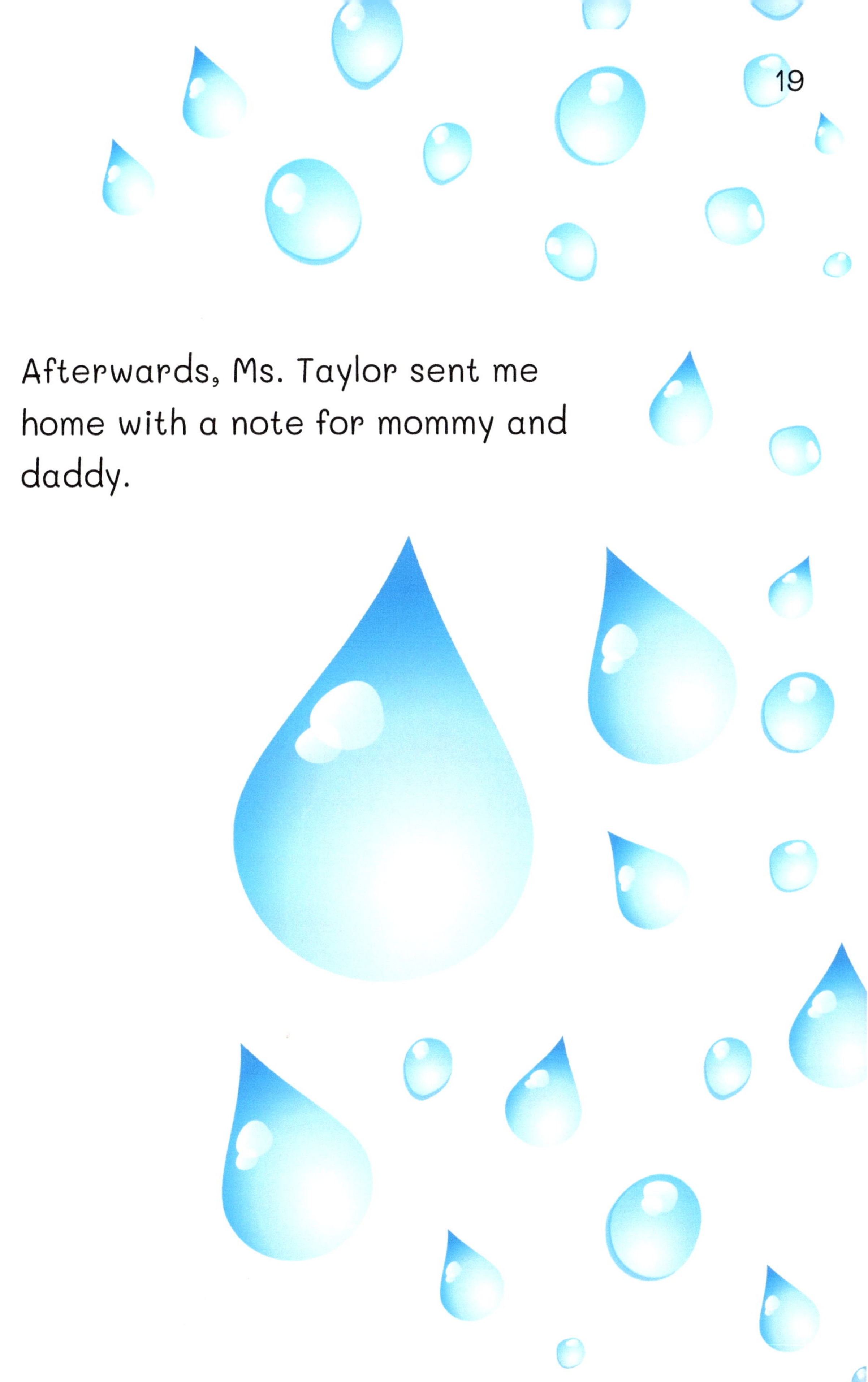

Afterwards, Ms. Taylor sent me home with a note for mommy and daddy.

"What did the note say?" Bibi asked.

"It said that Afrocentric hairstyles were not acceptable for ballerinas. My teacher even made a list of other hair styles I can't wear. It included **Bantu knots**, **box braids**, **cornrows**, and **Fulani braids**," Ninoshka added.

Bibi was furious about how Ninoshka had been treated, but she also understood how her granddaughter felt.

"Do you really need to straighten your hair?" Bibi asked.

"Yes, because I want to put my hair in a beautiful **sleek bun** like the other ballerinas."

Ninoshka paused, looked up curiously at Bibi, and asked, "Why doesn't my hair look like everyone else's, Bibi?"

"Because you are different!" Bibi said proudly.

"But I don't want to be different. I want to be like everyone else!" Ninoshka exclaimed.

Bibi responded, "You are a Black girl and, most importantly, you are an *African girl*! It's natural for your hair to have a unique texture."

"But Mandy, my classmate, is also African and her hair is straight," Ninoshka said.

"I think Mandy's parents relax her hair," Bibi explained.

"Can you relax my hair, too?"
Ninoshka asked.

"Apana ('no'). Your mother and I believe you are too young to straighten your hair. If you still want to when you're older, then that's your decision."

"Until then, we want you to embrace your natural hair," Bibi said firmly.

"It's just not fair! Why?"
Ninoshka blurted.

"Listen to me, Ninoshka.
You are a masterpiece.

Why would I change a masterpiece?"

Every coil, kink, and curl was created with perfection in mind. "You are living art, and why would I change that about you?"

Look at your brown skin!
Look at your bold hair! It
sprouts from your head like
a **mighty oak tree**.

And why would I want to change that?

"What should I say when they call my hair
'messy' or 'ugly'?"
Ninoskha asked.

"Tell them that your hair is your crown! Like
a *tiger's stripes*, each strand on your head
is special, and that is what
makes you beautiful,"
Bibi encouraged.

"If you say so," Ninoshka sulked.

"What's the matter, Ninoshka? **Why are you still sad?**"

"Bibi, I don't want to go back. I don't want to be a ballerina anymore!" Ninoshka shouted.

"Look into this mirror and tell me what you see," Bibi said.

Ninoshka stepped closer to the mirror.

"I see nothing," Ninoshka replied.

"Angalia tena ('look again')," Bibi urged her.

"*I see me*," Ninoshka sighed.

"When I was picked on as a child, my Bibi taught me this affirmation and it went like this, can you repeat after me?"

"I am beautiful just the way I am.
I believe I am beautiful.
I know I am.
My skin glows like gold.
My hair is my crown.
I wear it with pride.
From my roots to the ground."

Ninoshka repeated after Bibi and nodded with a smile.

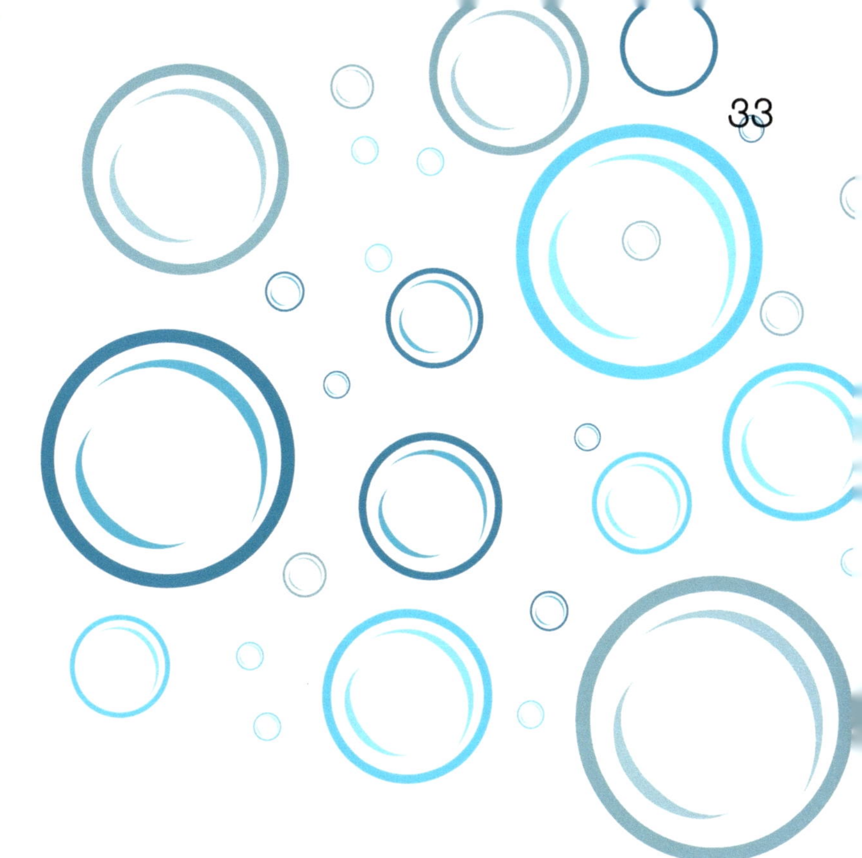

"That's my girl! Now let's wash your hair so you can go to bed. Tomorrow your parents and I will make some phone calls to see what we can do about this problem you've been having in ballet class," Bibi comforted her.

The next day Bibi walked into Ninoshka's room and gave her a ballet leotard.

"Aww, do I have to?" Ninoshka asked.

"Yes, it's time for you to go back to ballet class. Put on your leotard and tutu, and get ready!" Bibi ordered.

"Bibi, what am I going to do with my hair?"
she asked as she looked at her afro in
her bedroom mirror.

"Leave it," Bibi said with a smile.

"But my teacher said that
my hair has to be worn in a
sleek bun."

Ninoshka, look in the mirror and tell me what you see," Bibi said patiently.

"I see me," Ninoshka said gazing at her reflection.

"Good! Do you want to know what I see? I see a beautiful ballerina. I've watched you dance and you are magical in the way you move! Your talent is what makes a good ballerina, not your hair.

In class, Ms. Taylor's job is to teach you how to glisser gracefully and be the best ballerina you can be. At home, our job is to help teach you how to discover and love who you are, just as you are. Unanisikia ('Do you hear me')?"

Ninoshka nodded.

Bibi smiled and said,
"Okay, twende ('let's go')!"

When Ninoshka arrived at her dance class, everything was different.
"Where is everybody?"

"Well, your mother and I made a call to your ballet school. Sometimes, it takes one person taking a stand to see change. Yes, the normal rule is for a ballerina to wear a sleek bun, but sometimes old rules have to make room for something new and exceptional!

Ninoshka, YOU are exceptional and the world is able to change for little girls like you. I want you to remember this: no one has the right to tell you who you should be!"

Bibi continued, "You are the only one who can decide who you will be and what you can achieve. Your parents and I will do everything we can to make this world a better place for you while you're young. Until then, don't ever give up on yourself or the things you love because you are different, unanisikia ('do you hear me')?"

Yes — I do, Bibi!" Ninoshka quipped.

When Ninoshka's ballet instructor entered the room, Ninoshka gasped.

"Bibi, look! My new teacher looks like me.

Her hair looks like mine, too!"

"Ninoshka, I encourage you to find places where you are **celebrated** for who you are, kinks, coils, and all! As long as you work hard, you can do anything!" Bibi said heartily.

Ninoshka walked across the classroom and stood right in front of the wide mirror.

Then she recited her new affirmation as her grandmother walked away with an upbeat stride. Her new classmates watched in awe as she declared...

"I, Ninoshka, know that I am beautiful.
I am beautiful just the way that I am."

Help Ninoshka say her affirmation!
Fill your name on the blank line
and repeat the words.

I, _______________________________, know that I am
beautiful. I am beautiful just the way that I am.
My skin glows gloriously in the sun.
My crown is coiled and always fun
Whether braided, twisted, in a 'fro or a bun.
I wear it with pride as I step and I stride.
I am bold, I am beautiful.
That starts deep inside!

My hair, it sprouts like the roots
Of a mighty tree.
It blossoms like wildflowers
In a meadow that runs deep.
My hair has roots that stem
From my scalp to the palm of my hand.
That's what makes me special,
Just like every strand.
My hair's thick and strong like a lion's mane!
It makes me who I am, as unique as my name!

I know that I'm beautiful just the way that I am!
I know that I'm beautiful, I know that I am!

The end.